Scarlatti Masterpieces

for Solo Piano

47 Works

Domenico Scarlatti

DOVER PUBLICATIONS, INC.
Mineola, New York

Bibliographical Note

This Dover edition, first published in 1999, is a selection of sonatas from *D. Scarlatti, Opere complete per clavicembalo,* edited by Alessandro Longo, as published in eleven volumes, 1906–08, by G. Ricordi & C., Milan. The annotated table of contents and note have been prepared specially for the present edition.

International Standard Book Number

ISBN-13: 978-0-486-40851-4
ISBN-10: 0-486-40851-5

Manufactured in the United States by Courier Corporation
40851508   2015
www.doverpublications.com

Note

This Dover edition of Domenico Scarlatti's keyboard sonatas reprints the musical texts from the edition prepared by Alessandro Longo in 1906–08. Scholarly research in more recent times has shed considerable light on keyboard practice in the Baroque era. It is obvious that the Longo edition, pioneering and monumental though it was, preceded such research and did not have its advantages. Longo conceived his edition for performance by the piano in place of the original instrument, the harpsichord. The edition thus includes traditional pianistic markings—the use of pedal, slurs, staccati, dynamics, including crescendi and diminuendi—as well as ornamentation now generally considered inappropriate; moreover, Longo's absolute indications of tempi were foreign to Scarlatti. The suggestions of phrasing and contrasting dynamics lie within the music itself rather than through explicit indication.

This is not to suggest that these sonatas can be played only on the harpsichord, but the performer on the piano should endeavor to approach the historical style as closely as possible. In the interest of providing an affordable edition, however, the pianistic elements of phrasing, dynamics, and pedal remain as they appear in the Longo edition. (The actual notation—pitches and lengths—is reliable and beautifully engraved.)

The performer desiring to understand more fully the interpretation of these sonatas is urged to consult the definitive study, *Domenico Scarlatti*, by the distinguished harpsichordist and scholar Ralph Kirkpatrick (Princeton University Press, 1953; paperback edition published by Thomas Y. Crowell, 1968), with particular attention to chapter 12, pages 280–323, on "The Performance of the Scarlatti Sonatas."

In this Dover edition, three numbers are assigned to each sonata in both the contents list and below the heading on the music page: its Kirkpatrick [K] number; followed by its Longo [L] number (from Alessandro Longo, ed., *D. Scarlatti, Opere complete per clavicembalo*, Milan, 1906–08); then by its Pestelli [P] number (from Giorgio Pestelli, *Le sonate di Domenico Scarlatti: proposta di un ordinamento cronologico*, Turin, 1967).

The statement at the end of each sonata—in full or abbreviated C.V., C.S., or E.O.—indicates Longo's source for the musical text. His edition was based on three sources: (1) a manuscript copy made by a Spanish scribe—designated "C.V." for *Codice Veneziano*; (2) Italian copies in the Santini Collection, designated "C.S." for *Codice Santini*; and (3) the edition of thirty sonatas published in London in 1738 under the title *Essercizi per gravicembalo*—designated "E.O." for *Edizione Originale*.

CONTENTS

• The numbers accompanying each title refer to catalogs of Scarlatti's works compiled by Ralph Kirkpatrick ("K") (1953), Alessandro Longo ("L") (1906–08), and Giorgio Pestelli ("P") (1967). Only the "K" numbers are listed in chronological order. • Titles marked * are paginated out of sequence to preserve good page turns. • Sonatas marked † are considered by *Grove* to be of doubtful authenticity. • A subtitle in quotation marks is a popular reference to that work. • Incipits are reprinted from the Longo edition.

Scarlatti Masterpieces

Sonata in G major

K2 / L388 / P58

E. O., N. 2.

Sonata in D minor

("Pastorale")

K9 / L413 / P65

Sonata in C minor

K11 / L352 / P67

EDIZIONE ORIGINALE, N. II.

2 — E.O. a)   10 — E.O. b)   24 — E.O. c)

Sonata in E major

K20 / L375 / P76

Sonata in B minor

K27 / L449 / P83

E. O. N. 27.

Sonata in G minor

("Cat's Fugue")

K30 / L499 / P86

(145)

(150)

114 - E. O.

a)

139 - 147 E. O.

b)

152 - c) Nell' E. O l'ultimo accordo dura un movimento senza ⌢
  Dans l' E. O. le dernier accord dure un temps sans ⌢

Questa celebre composizione di D. S. è conosciuta col titolo di « Fuga del gatto » a causa dello strano procedimento degl'intervalli del tema. Si narra, che la prima idea del pezzo sia venuta all'A. dalle note toccate un giorno dalle zampe del suo gatto favorito. Il gustoso aneddoto è verosimile; ma il titolo caratteristico non appare nell'E. O. Lo si legge la prima volta nella vecchia collezione di Clementi « Practical Harmony ».

Cette célèbre composition de D. S. est connue sous le nom « La Fugue du chat » à cause de la marche étrange des intervalles du thème. On raconte que la première idée de ce morceau soit venue à l'A. des notes touchées un jour par les pattes de son chat favori. L'anecdoteg racieuse est vraisemblable, mais le titre caractéristique n'apparaît pas dans l'E. O. On le trouve pour la première fois dans l' ancienne collection de Clementi « Practical Harmony ».

En la E. O. el último acorde tiene el valor de una parte sin ⌢
In the E. O. the final chord lasts a movement without ⌢

Esta célebre composición de D. S. se conoce con el título « Fuga del gato » a causa del extraño procedimiento de los intervalos de su tema. Cuéntase que la primera idea de la pieza fuera sugerida al A. por las notas pisadas, un día, por su gato favorito. La graciosa anécdota es verosímil; pero el título característico no aparece en la E. O. Se lée por primera vez en la antigua colección Clementi « Practical Harmony ».

This celebrated composition of D. S. is known by the title of « Fugue of the cat » owing to the strange proceeding of the intervals of the theme. It is related, that the first idea the author had for the piece was given by the notes played one day by his favorite cat. The story is probable and very good: but the characteristic title does not appear in the E. O. It is read for the first time in the old collection of Clementi « Practical Harmony ».

24 / G minor, K30 *("Cat's Fugue")*

Sonata in D minor
(Aria)
K32 / L423 / P14

Sonata in D major

K33 / L424 / P130

C.V. Libro XIV, N. 43. (i)

Sonata in D minor

K34 / L S7 [Supplement] / P15

Sonata in C minor
(Minuetto)

K40 / L357 / P119

Sonata in B-flat major

K47 / L46 / P115

C.V. Libro XIV, N.5. *(i)*

a) C.V. *Presto*

Sonata in A minor

K54 / L241 / P147

C. V. Libro XIV, N. 12. *(e)*

Sonata in B minor

K87 / L33 / P43

C. V. Libro XIV, N. 52. *(i)*

Le scorrettezze del **C. V.** sono in questo pezzo assai numerose e spesso enigmatiche. Ne trascrivo due soltanto perchè si possa giudicare del metodo di correzione.

Les incorrections du C. V. sont fort nombreuses et souvent énigmatiques dans ce morceau. Je n'en transcris que deux afin qu'on puisse se rendre compte du système de correction.

Las incorrecciones del C. V. son en ésta pieza bastante numerosas y a menudo enigmáticas. Transcribo dos solamente, para que se pueda juzgar el método de corrección.

The errors of the C. V. in this piece are very numerous and often inexplicable. I transcribe two only in order that it may be judged of the method of correction.

11 — 12

37 — 38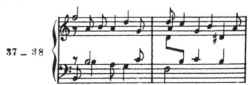

Sonata in D minor

(Gavotta)

K64 / L58 / P33

C. V. Libro XIV, N. 24.(*i*)

Sonata in C major

K95 / L358 / [unlisted by Pestelli]

C. S. Libro VII, N. 39. *(e)*

6 (e 14) C. S. *a)*   12 _ C. S. *b)*   13 _ C. S. *c)*

22 _ C. S. *d)*

25 - *e)* Questa misura manca nel C. S.   *Este compás falta en el C. S.*

Cette mesure manque dans le C. S.   This bar is missing in the C. V.

Sonata in D major

K96 / L465 / P210

C. V. Libro II, N. 6. (e)

26 - (e simili)   (y similes)   a) Figurazione del C. V.   *Figuración del C. V.*
   (et semblables) (and similar)   *Notation du C. V.*   Figuration of the C. V.

48-56 (e 121-124, 127-129)

   b) Nel C. V. mancano le legature di valore.   *En el C. V. faltan las ligaduras de valores.*
   Dans le C. V. les liaisons de valeur manquent. In the C. V. the ties of value are missing.

68 (e 75) – C. V. c) 𝄢

Sonata in A major

K101 / L494 / P156

C. S., Libro I, N. 29. e VII, N. 32. *(i)*

Sonata in A major

K113 / L345 / P160

C. V. Libro XV, N. 16. (e)

Sonata in C major

K159 / L104 / P418

17 – a) Questa misura manca nel C. V.   *Este compás falta en el C. V.*
   Cette mesure manque dans le C. V.   This bar is missing in the C. V.

Sonata in A-flat major

K127 / L186 / P198

C. V. Libro XV, N. 30. *(e)*

Sonata in C major

K132 / L457 / P295

C. V. Libro XV, N. 35. (e)

40 (e 41) - C. V. *a)*   77 - C. V. *b)*

Sonata in E major

K135 / L224 / P234

19-21 – a) Nel C. V. manca il ♮ al *Sol*.
Dans le C. V. le ♮ manque au Sol.

En el C. V. falta el ♮ al Sol.
In the C. V. the ♮ to *G* is missing.

33 – b) Nel C. V. questa misura è ripetuta; ma è evidente che
il frammento 32-38 dev'essere simile al 25-31.
*Dans le C. V. cette mesure est répétée; mais sans doute
le fragment 32-38 doit être semblable à celui 25-31.*

*En el C. V. este compás esta repetido; pero es evidente que el
fragmento 32-38 debe ser semejante al 25-31.*
In the C. V. this bar is repeated but it is evident that the
fragment 32-38 has to be similar to 25-31.

Sonata in G major

K146 / L349 / P106

Dal Volume 148 (32 F. 13) del « Fitzwilliam Museum » di Cambridge, N. 7. (i).

Du Volume 148 (32 F 13) du « Fitzwilliam Museum » de Cambridge, N. 7. (i).

Del Volumen 148 (32 F 13) del « Fitzwilliam Museum » di Cambridge, N. 7. (i).

From Volume 148 (32 F 13) of the « Fitzwilliam Museum » of Cambridge, N. 7. (i).

Sonata in A minor

K149 / L93 / P241

C. V. Libro I, N. 2. (i)

Sonata in E major

K162 / L21 / P162

C.V. Libro I, N. 15. (i)

Sonata in F minor

K184 / L189 / P102

C. V. Libro II, N. 8. *(i)*

7 _ C. V.

Sonata in A minor

K175 / L429 / P136

Sonata in E minor

K198 / L22 / P132

C.V. Libro II, N. 27.(i)

Sonata in A major

K208 / L238 / P315

C. V. Libro III, N. 3. *(i)*

Sonata in C-sharp minor

K247 / L256 / P297

C. V. Libro IV, N. 12. (e)

Sonata in F-sharp major

K319 / L35 / P303

Sonata in G major

K260 / L124 / P304

110

C. V. Libro IV, N. 25. (e)

17-20 – C. V.   a)   82 (e 87, 185, 190) – b)

Formule du trille: Fórmula del trino:
Formula del trillo: Formula of the trill:

Sonata in A major

K322 / L483 / P360

C. V. Libro VI, N. 27. *(l)*

Sonata in E major
(Capriccio)

K380 / L23 / P483

C.V. Libro VIII, N.23 . (*i*)

Sonata in G major

K338 / L87 / P400

C. V. Libro VII, N. 13. (i)

Sonata in E minor

K402 / L427 / P496

C.V. Libro IX, N. 15. (i)

Sonata in G major

K427 / L286 / P464

C. V. Libro X, N. 10. (e)

1 - a) Nel C. V. è scritto: « *Presto quanto sia possibile* ».   En el C. V. está escrito: « Presto cuanto sea posible ».
     Dans le C. V. il est écrit: « Aussi vite que possibile ».   In the C. V. is written: « *As quickly as possible* ».

Sonata in D major
("Balletto")

K430 / L463 / P329

C. V. Libro X, N. 13. *(e)*

Sonata in B-flat major
(Minuetto)
K440 / L97 / P328

C. V. Libro X, N. 23. *(i)*

Sonata in G major

K431 / L83 / P365

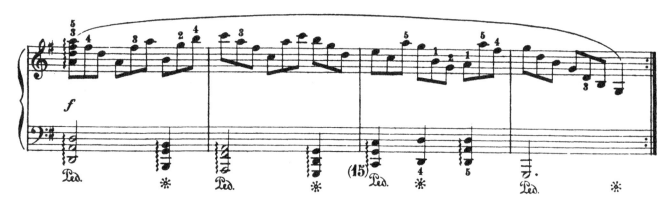

Sonata in F minor

K466 / L118 / P501

ANDANTE MODERATO (♩ = 96)

C. V. Libro XI, N. 13. (i)

Sonata in E-flat major

K474 / L203 / P502

C. V. Libro XI, N. 21. (e)

148 / E-flat major, K474

Sonata in F minor

K481 / L187 / P504

C. V. Libro XI, N. 28. *(e)*

Sonata in D major

K491 / L164 / P484

154 / D major, K491

C. V. Libro XII, N. 8. *(i)*   1 – C. V. ^a) *ALLEGRO*

1 (e 2) – *b*) Formula del gruppetto : *Fórmula del grupeto:* Formula of the turn:

Formule du gruppetto:

22 (e 65) – *c*) Formula del gruppetto : *Fórmula del grupeto:*

Formule du gruppetto: Formula of the turn :

Sonata in C major
(Pastorale)
K513 / L S3 [Supplement] / P176

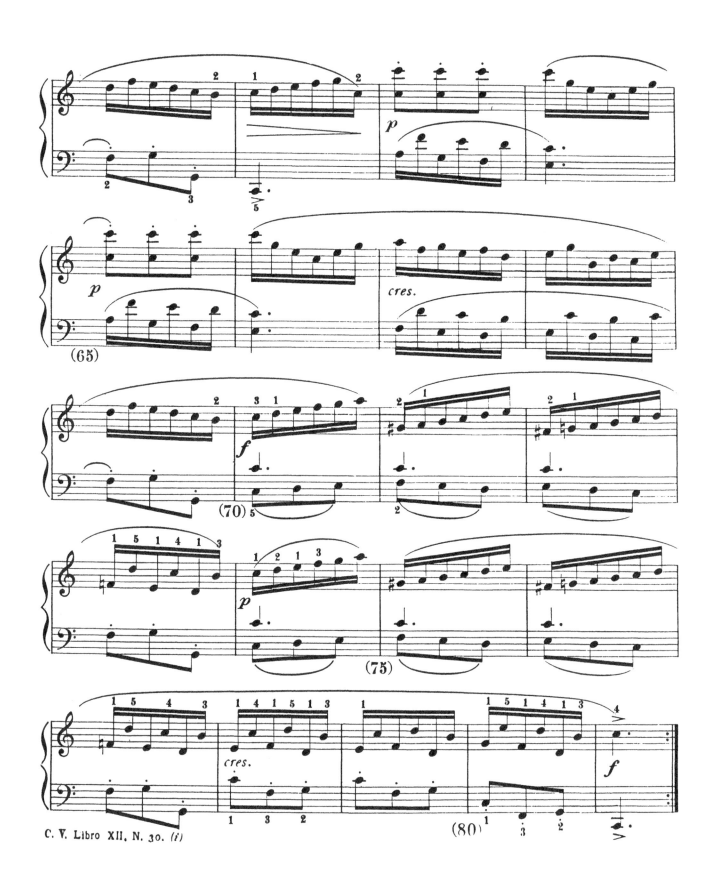

Sonata in F major

K525 / L188 / P529

C. V. Libro XIII, N. 12. (e) (70)

23 -(e 29 - 31)_C. V.

a)

La correzione è fatta sul modello delle misure 69 e 71.

La correction est faite suivant le modèle des mesures 69 et 71.

La correción está hecha inspirada en el modelo de los compases 69 y 71.

The correction is made on the model of bars 69 and 71.

Sonata in E major

K531 / L430 / P535

END OF EDITION